Finding Strength in the Pursuit

FINDING
Strength
IN THE
PURSUIT

30 daily devotionals to strengthen, enccurage and ignite women tc pursue their God giver destinies

MANDY KENNEY

XULON PRESS

Xulon Press
2301 Lucien Way #415
Maitland, FL 32751
407.339.4217
www.xulonpress.com

© 2018 by Mandy Kenney

All rights reserved solely by the author. The author guarantees all contents are original and do not infringe upon the legal rights of any other person or work. No part of this book may be reproduced in any form without the permission of the author. The views expressed in this book are not necessarily those of the publisher.

Unless otherwise indicated, Scripture quotations taken from the English Standard Version (ESV). Copyright © 2001 by Crossway, a publishing ministry of Good News Publishers. Used by permission. All rights reserved.

Scripture quotations taken from the New King James Version (NKJV). Copyright © 1982 by Thomas Nelson, Inc. Used by permission. All rights reserved.

Scripture quotations taken from the Holy Bible, New Living Translation (NLT). Copyright ©1996, 2004, 2007 by Tyndale House Foundation. Used by permission of Tyndale House Publishers, Inc.

Scripture quotations taken from The Message (MSG). Copyright © 1993, 1994, 1995, 1996, 2000, 2001, 2002. Used by permission of NavPress Publishing Group. Used by permission. All rights reserved.

Printed in the United States of America.

ISBN-13: 978-1-54564-399-0

Dedication

For my dad who is already with Jesus. Before he left this earth, he taught me what it meant to seek Jesus. May his legacy of choosing Him live on through the words in this book and through my life.

For my husband, Brad who encourages me like no one else. Who believes in me and keeps me grounded at all times. He is my greatest gift in life, and I love him with everything in me.

For my son, Braycen, and my daughter, Payten. My beautiful children that God entrusted me to raise. Being their Mom is one of the highest honors I have in life.

Table of Contents

Dedication v
Introduction ix

DAY 1:   What's Your Purpose? 1
DAY 2:   What's Your Response? 3
DAY 3:   Free Access 5
DAY 4:   What's Your Distraction? 7
DAY 5:   Pillars in a Palace 9
DAY 6:   Rivers of Life 11
DAY 7:   Shaped by God 13
DAY 8:   Perspective Change 15
DAY 9:   May God Be Glorified 19
DAY 10: Encourage in a Storm 21
DAY 11: Growth 25
DAY 12: Kingdom Builders 27
DAY 13: Control Fear 29
DAY 14: The Fiery Furnace 33
DAY 15: Choose Your Path 37
DAY 16: Miracles in Obedience 41
DAY 17: Trust 45
DAY 18: Hope 49
DAY 19: Get Away 51

Finding Strength in the Pursuit

DAY 20: Proclaim His Name 55
DAY 21: Little Faith 59
DAY 22: Idle 63
DAY 23: Holy 65
DAY 24: The Trap of Pride 67
DAY 25: Faithfulness 71
DAY 26: The Word 75
DAY 27: Passion or Perfection? 77
DAY 28: Our Hearts 79
DAY 29: Use Your Voice 81
DAY 30: Fan Your Flame 83

Conclusion 85
Acknowledgments 87
Notes 89

Introduction

I grew up in a Christian home, but it wasn't until after I tested the waters that I fully surrendered my life to Jesus. I lived a life that many can relate to. I had one foot in the world and one foot in the church. I thought I could still worship Jesus by attending church and praying occasionally, yet still live my life on the weekends and do whatever I wanted to do. But, true fulfillment didn't occur in my life until I fully surrendered everything to follow Him. *"Then Jesus said to his disciples, "If any of you wants to be my follower, you must give up your own way, take up your cross, and follow me"* (Matthew 16:24; NLT).

I came to a place in my life where I wanted God more than I wanted to get drunk and go to the bars every weekend with friends. I wanted to know more about Him—even though I was taught at a young age who He was—I didn't know Him personally. When I finally stopped living a life of my own, I found true fulfillment. I found my worth in Jesus, and I learned how He loved me and why He died for me. I found what gifts God had given me to build His kingdom and how I was supposed to use them to help others see that they too have been set apart.

True freedom comes when we realize our life isn't our own. That we have a purpose that is greater than just for ourselves.

Jesus died so that we could be free. He loves us so much that He gave His life so that we could have a life of total fulfillment. My only response to His extravagant love toward me was and still is—full surrender.

During the pursuit of finding who we are in Jesus, we will hit roadblocks. We will encounter storms and trials, but there is strength found in Jesus, His written word, and His grace. As you pursue more of Him, He will leave you encouraged and strengthened, but we must be relentless in our pursuit. Our lives are like a race. A slow race, but one that requires us to be consistent and never give up. Galatians 6:9 says, *"And let us not grow weary in doing good, for in due season we will reap, if we do not give up"* (ESV).

I pray that these devotionals catapult you into a life of full surrender and leave you hungry for more of God's word. That you'll live in reckless faith and understanding that you are a daughter of the King who has placed a mantle of great purpose on your life. The gifts and talents that God has given you will bring glory to Him and bring many others into the kingdom.

You've already begun your journey of the pursuit by picking up this book. Let's see what God has in store for you based on that simple act!

DAY 1

WHAT'S YOUR PURPOSE?

ACTS 14:1-28

In your everyday life, you may have times of wanting to throw in the towel. The challenges and the hurdles make you feel like it's too hard to persevere. But, I want to show you how Paul got back up after being knocked down—almost dead. The key to his perseverance was knowing his purpose.

In Acts chapter 14 it talks of Paul being stoned. I felt so shocked and in awe when I read it. The Jews stoned him with the intent to kill him. When they thought he was dead, they dragged him out of the city. Imagine that scene for a moment. Being stoned is so violent. It's horrific. Paul was unconscious with blood present on his clothes, and perhaps he was barely taking breaths if they thought he was dead. He was drug out of the city and they left his body… But, it wasn't over.

As the disciples gathered around him, Paul gets up, enters the city, and leaves the very next day with Barnabas to Derbe. Did you catch that? He got up! Then, he returned to where he started at Lystra after he preached in Derbe. Verse 22 tells us that he *"Strengthened the souls of the disciples, encouraging them to continue in the faith, and saying that through many tribulations we must enter the kingdom of God."*

Paul knew his purpose. He was called by God to accomplish His will. With the power of the Holy Spirit, Paul got back up and continued on his journey. But, he didn't just keep the finish line in his vision: he focused on the now. He didn't just go through the motions to get to the end: he fought; he persevered; and, he focused on the assignment that he had in that moment.

There are times in my life that the situation in the middle seems too overwhelming to try and tackle. I have life screaming at me and every person in my family calling my name. They need me to help with homework, a school project, clean uniforms for their sports, a husband that needs encouragement after a long week of struggles, my family needing groceries, etc. The list goes on. But, in my fatigue, and in my weariness, and almost dead state of mind, I focus on God. I focus on what He's called me to do, and I know He will be with me and strengthen me.

Let's be like Paul. Let's risk it all for the kingdom of God. When we're half dead, exhausted, and burned out from life, let's get back up and give God the glory as we pursue His will and agenda. It's not over.

DAY 2

WHAT'S YOUR RESPONSE?

My response to bumps in the road, or hiccups in life, will show where my trust is. It will prove where my faith lies. And if I'm honest, many times I'm not happy with my response to life's challenges. We really have two choices when we face struggles, don't we? Either we choose joy or we choose despair.

In Acts we are shown how Paul and Silas handle a bump in the road. They were thrown into prison for casting out a demon in a girl. They had their feet shackled after they had just been beaten with rods and received many blows to their body. Now, they're in prison, in pain, and another road block is thrown into their path of preaching the gospel.

How did they respond? *"About midnight Paul and Silas were praying and singing hymns to God, and the prisoners were listening to them"* (Acts 16:25; ESV).

If you continue reading, scripture tells us that an earthquake erupts and the jail doors burst open leaving everyone's shackles unfastened. The guard was so afraid that he would receive a horrible punishment from allowing them to escape, that he was about to take his own life. Paul stops him and tells him they're all still there.

The guard's response? *"Then he brought them out and said, 'Sirs, what must I do to be saved?'"* (Acts 16:30; ESV). He saw how Paul and Silas handled this road block. He saw how they prayed and worshiped God. He saw them have peace and hope in Jesus, even when their circumstances took a different turn. He saw the miracle-working God through Paul and Silas, and he wanted that kind of God in his own life.

The end of this story explains that the guard and his whole household were saved and baptized. All of them! Could this have happened if Paul and Silas's response was different? If they would have been in a state of defeat? Moping around, feeling hopeless based on their situation, because, after all, they would have been justified in those actions? They were in prison for goodness sake! But, they used their situation to give God the glory and changed an entire family's legacy by their response.

Could your response and the way you worship God be bringing others into the kingdom? Let's show others Jesus and the hope we have in Him by the way we respond.

DAY 3

FREE ACCESS

Have you ever tried to walk blindfolded? You can't see a thing in front of you, so you try to feel things with your hands and feet and move ever so slowly. You don't know what lies ahead because your eyes are covered. This is similar to what happens when we get caught up in life issues. We can't see anything in front of us except that blindfold. We're left with uncertainty and worry about what lies ahead because we forget that we can take off the blindfold. When we accepted Jesus into our hearts, He removed that blindfold, but sometimes we put it back on without knowing.

> *So if you're serious about living this new resurrection life with Christ, act like it. Pursue the things over which Christ presides. Don't shuffle along, eyes to the ground, absorbed with the things right in front of you. Look up, and be alert to what is going on around Christ—that's where the action is. See things from his perspective.* (Colossians 3:1-2; MSG)

It's easy to get lost in our own circumstances and miss an opportunity to see things clearly. When we're absorbed with our own lives and our own problems, we get distracted from our mission, or our next step. I see this picture of someone hiking in the woods. They've traveled for days and ran out of water earlier that day. They're still a hundred miles from camp, and they've become so thirsty that they've started looking for water under any rocks along the trail. They have become so focused on a few pebbles providing dampened dirt that they miss the slow-moving creek next to them. Isn't that how we live sometimes? Completely focused on the one thing we think we need, and miss out on the free access Jesus has already given us?

If you have your blindfold on today, I encourage you to remove it, and see things the way Jesus does. Look up! Be alert to what's going on with a kingdom mindset. Another translation says, *"Set your minds on things that are above, not on things that are on earth"* (Colossians 3:2). That's where the action is friends. That's where the free access resides. Let's live in that perspective.

DAY 4

WHAT'S YOUR DISTRACTION?

So often, feelings can be deceiving. Especially for women in the roller coaster of hormones we have some months. Your husband forgets to say he loves you on the way out the door, and you think the worst. Your boss calls you into the office to go over something, and you think you're getting fired. You have a bad hair day, and you think everyone at the store is looking at you like a drowned rat. Am I the only one?

I recently had a rough week, and if I can be real with you, that distracted me from my gift. For a couple days, I was dwelling on the failed expectations I had placed on people. The enemy twisted it and I was left feeling insecure, inadequate, and unloved.

But, I powered through those feelings with my eyes trying to focus on the truth. I knew I was being deceived. I knew it was the enemy lying to me, but it took a lot of effort and prayer to get my mind to line up with my spirit. Did you catch that? It took a lot of effort to get myself back to where I needed to be.

My distractions removed me from my post. The enemy was distracting me, so that he could walk in through the front gate of whatever I was "watching" over in prayer. Why? Because I wasn't alert and being watchful. I was consumed with my feelings. I lost sight of my mission and my assignment because I was so focused on my feelings and the lack of follow through I expected from people.

I lost my confidence in my gift and what I was called to do. The enemy took me down a rabbit trail that would have led to death spiritually if I didn't stop it. He wanted to keep me distracted, so I wouldn't fulfill the call God placed on me. Maybe that's where you are right now.

> *"Therefore do not throw away your confidence, which has a great reward. For you have need of endurance, so that when you have done the will of God you may receive what is promised"* (Hebrews 10:35-36; ESV).

God wants you to use your gifts. He gave them to you. He created you to further His kingdom with what He placed inside of you. It takes endurance; it takes confidence; and, it takes faith. Whatever God has planted inside you is good. Don't get distracted. Be mindful of the enemy's tricks and be in prayer. God chose YOU to fulfill His plan to further His kingdom.

DAY 5

PILLARS IN A PALACE

When we have guests coming over to our house, we go into a military mode. I give my kids chores, and I spend a couple hours getting the house clean and spotless. Because that's really how we all live, right? Homes are clean and spotless all the time? My kids will ask, "Why are we cleaning if it's just going to get messy when they come over?" I don't know kids. It's just what we're supposed to do.

But, in reality, my heart is to provide a place where my guests feel comfortable and honored. A place where they can sit back and relax and enjoy the company of their friends and family. I even like to think that it provides a joyful atmosphere to everyone.

> *May our sons flourish in their youth like well-nurtured plants. May our daughters be like graceful pillars, carved to beautify a palace. May our barns be filled with crops of every kind. May the flocks in our fields multiply by the thousands, even tens of thousands, and may our oxen be loaded down with produce. May*

> *there be no enemy breaking through our walls, no going into captivity, no cries of alarm in our town squares. Yes, joyful are those who live like this! Joyful indeed are those whose God is the Lord.* (Psalms 144:12-15; NLT)

Another translation says, *"Our daughters are like corner pillars cut for the structure of a palace."*

We are pillars in our homes, in the church, and in our workplaces because we have been cut and sculpted into place by our King, our Creator. He has purposefully placed us there because He knows our husbands, our children, our friends, strangers, and coworkers need a palace that hosts the Holy Spirit.

Now, shift your thoughts onto your inner man from a physical structure. Your spirit. You are the palace. The temple of God. The place where the Holy Spirit resides is in you. The physical palace is your spirit. You carry the Holy Spirit with you and provide a palace for Him. And the result, scripture tells us, is joy! The end of the passage says, *"Joyful are those that live like this!"*

Whether our minds line up with this truth every moment of the day, or once a week, it doesn't change it from being true. Let's choose joy this week as we host the King of kings in our palace.

DAY 6

RIVERS OF LIFE

On the final and climactic day of the Feast Jesus took his stand. He cried out, "If anyone thirsts, let him come to me and drink. Rivers of living water will brim and spill out of the depths of anyone who believes in me this way, just as the Scripture says." (He said this in regard to the Spirit, whom those who believed in him were about to receive. The Spirit had not yet been given because Jesus had not yet been glorified., (John 7:37-39 MSG)

This passage describes the coming of the Holy Spirit. Jesus hadn't yet been crucified, but He was describing to His people how essential the Holy Spirit was going to be after He was no longer physically on earth.

What was the result of receiving the Holy Spirit? Scripture says rivers of living water will brim and spill out of the depths of anyone who believes in Him.

All through the scriptures we hear of the living water Jesus talks about. It quenches areas of our lives and depths of our being that nothing else can quench. Not only does it satisfy us, but it produces the fruit in our lives. How else can fruit grow, but by being watered daily. Let the Holy Spirit water you so you can produce fruit.

Now look what Revelation says:

> *Then the angel showed me the river of the water of life, bright as crystal, flowing from the throne of God and of the Lamb through the middle of the street of the city; also, on either side of the river, the tree of life with its twelve kinds of fruit, yielding its fruit each month. The leaves of the tree were for the healing of the nations.* (Revelation 22:1-2 ; ESV)

I believe we have that river of life flowing in us right now by the Holy Spirit. There may be days we tap into that water like an irrigation canal in our backyard, and there are days we are too tired to put effort into hauling those hoses and other resources to get that flow to change in our direction.

We need this water to survive. We need it to grow our fruit, which scripture tells us will come in due season.

Don't give up because you don't see the fruit yet. Keep tapping into the river of life! Even your leaves that you have can bring healing to the nations, as Revelation tells us, God uses everything. Even though your fruit may not be ripe for the picking yet, your leaves can bring healing to those around you!

DAY 7

SHAPED BY GOD

And that about wraps it up. God is strong, and he wants you strong. So take everything the Master has set out for you, well-made weapons of the best materials. And put them to use so you will be able to stand up to everything the Devil throws your way. This is no afternoon athletic contest that we'll walk away from and forget about in a couple of hours. This is for keeps, a life-or-death fight to the finish against the Devil and all his angels. (Ephesians 6:10-12; MSG)

We are at constant war with the enemy. But, when we are fully clothed in the armor, we are prepared. We are ready. When an army goes to battle, they're focused on their mission. Whether our mission is to war in the spirit, raise our children in God's Name, speak truth to a stranger, or even bring hope to a neighbor, the enemy will try to hinder us. Anything that builds God's kingdom, the enemy will try and stop.

There are many ways the enemy can attack us. For me, it's my worth. The enemy knows my weak spots. He has studied me for a long time, just like he has studied you. So our areas of weakness must be protected in a greater way.

> *So roll up your sleeves, put your mind in gear, be totally ready to receive the gift that's coming when Jesus arrives. Don't lazily slip back into those old grooves of evil, doing just what you feel like doing. You didn't know any better then; you do now. As obedient children, let yourselves be pulled into a way of life shaped by God's life, a life energetic and blazing with holiness. God said, "I am holy; you be holy."* (1 Peter 1:13-16; MSG)

Let's allow God's life to shape our life, rather than living in our insecurities and our low self-esteem. He is the reason we have life. If we keep reading verses 18-19 in 1 Peter, it says, *"Knowing that you were ransomed from the futile ways inherited from your forefathers, not with perishable things such as silver or gold, but with the precious blood of Christ, like that of a lamb without blemish or spot"* (ESV).

You were ransomed by the precious blood of Jesus. He bought you with His blood. When we keep Him in front, our lives mold into His, and soon we don't even see ourselves anymore. We only see Jesus.

DAY 8

PERSPECTIVE CHANGE

I live in a valley surrounded by mountains. I see them every day, and they're there whether I notice them or not. They can either look like a beautiful tapestry painted by God Himself or an obstacle that is hindering me from crossing over.

Sometimes, we think we have a mountain in front of us or one that we've been traveling around for decades. But, what if it's really a beautiful tapestry that is placed there to show us God's sovereign beauty?

> *"My suffering was good for me, for it taught me to pay attention to your decrees. Your instructions are more valuable to me than millions in gold and silver '* (Psalms 119:71-72 ; NLT).

When we talk about suffering, it's hard to consider we should be grateful for it. But, as we know, God works out all things together for good. He uses every single ounce of it for His glory. Your mountain that you're up against might be familiar to you. You might know the path around it like the back of your hand, or it might be a brand new one. Either way, the struggle is real. It's exhausting and can be defeating. James chooses to focus on the final outcome.

> *If your faith remains strong, even while surrounded by life's difficulties, you will continue to experience the untold blessings of God! True happiness comes as you pass the test with faith, and receive the victorious crown of life promised to every lover of God!* (James 1:12; TPT)

James urges us in his letter to choose joy, remain steadfast in faith, and to see things from a different perspective. I want to challenge you to shift your focus today if it's gotten you stuck on your obstacle. Can you shift it to see it as a tapestry?

> *"Write this letter to the angel of the church in Philadelphia. This is the message from the one who is holy and true, the one who has the key of David. What he opens, no one can close; and what he closes, no one can open."* (Revelation 3:7; NLT)

If we live with this understanding that God is in charge, our faith will rise. For nothing can stop the plans of God from unfolding in your life. As Revelation says, whatever God opens, no one can come along and shut it. And, if He shuts a door, you can't break it down; it doesn't matter how hard you try!

Be encouraged that God is for you. He's your protector and He could have painted a beautiful mountain in front of you to show off His sovereign plans for your life. God can take anything and make something beautiful.

> *To grant to those who mourn in Zion— to give them a beautiful headdress instead of ashes, the oil of gladness instead of mourning, the garment of praise instead of a faint spirit; that they may be called oaks of righteousness, the planting of the Lord, that he may be glorified.* (Isaiah 61:3; ESV)

DAY 9

MAY GOD BE GLORIFIED

As I was reading through the scriptures, something jumped out at me. As grandmas, moms, wives, sisters, aunts, and friends, we can juggle many different tasks and wear a variety of hats. There are days we feel like superwoman taking on five different tasks with our eyes closed while using our hands and feet like an octopus. Then there are days where we couldn't possibly add another thing to our plate and stay sane.

When we rest in our own abilities and our own agendas, we lose our drive. We lose the ability to juggle, and we forget why we are doing those things.

Have you ever asked yourself, *Why do I bother cleaning when my littles come behind me and spill food and drinks all over the floor and couch?* Or maybe you've said to yourself, *Why do I bother to pick up my husband's clothes off the floor when he is a grown man and can put them in the hamper himself?* (I may have muttered that one under my breath before.) We can quickly lose our mission when we take our eyes off of Jesus. Peter reminds us in scripture to keep love in the center of our motives.

Finding Strength in the Pursuit

> *Above all, keep loving one another earnestly, since love covers a multitude of sins. Show hospitality to one another without grumbling. As each has received a gift, use it to serve one another, as good stewards of God's varied grace: whoever speaks, as one who speaks oracles of God; whoever serves, as one who serves by the strength that God supplies—in order that in everything God may be glorified through Jesus Christ. To him belong glory and dominion forever and ever. Amen."* (1 Peter 4:8-11; ESV)

Show hospitality to one another without grumbling. Ouch! If we keep loving one another earnestly, it covers a multitude of sins. I need my sins covered! Anyone else?

So, when we don't feel like vacuuming again, picking up laundry again, or making dinner for our families, how do we do it in love? This passage tells us "in order that in everything God may be glorified." Everything.

That's how we show love with the gifts God has given us. We do it so that God gets the glory. Not us. We serve with the gifts God has given us, so that He will shine through us to others. And, scripture tells us God supplies our strength!

Keep loving others with everything in you. Keep loving people as if your life depended on it. God will get the glory when you keep Him the reason and the motive you serve and love His people.

DAY 10

Encourage in a Storm

Acts 27:13-38

Have you ever been in a physical storm or a spiritual storm? I have been in both, and it's frightening. It leaves me vulnerable in the frenzy of being out of control. I can't control anything but myself, and that doesn't bring much comfort. But, what happens when we take our storm and give thanks to God in the midst of it?

Let's pick up in Acts chapter 27. It was right after Paul was arrested and was being brought to Caesar as a prisoner. He was on a ship with guards and other prisoners when a great storm rose against them. They became so afraid they started throwing cargo and food overboard. The text tells us an angel came to Paul and told him what to say.

> *Yet now I urge you to take heart, for there will be no loss of life among you, but only of the ship. For this very night there stood before me an angel of the God to whom I belong and whom I worship, and he said, "Do not be afraid,*

> *Paul; you must stand before Caesar. And behold, God has granted you all those who sail with you." So take heart, men, for I have faith in God that it will be exactly as I have been told. But we must run aground on some island.* (Acts 27:22-26; ESV)

Look what God told him. Not only did He cover the fear that Paul was carrying about meeting with Caesar, but God provided a word for Paul's fellow passengers. A word of hope.

In the middle of our storms, God is faithful to give us a word of hope, but if we listen closely, He will give a word of hope for someone else as well. Keep other people close to your heart when you spend time with Jesus. He will give you the words of encouragement that they need right in the middle of a storm.

Watch what happens when Paul focuses on God, his mission, and what he was called to do.

> *Therefore I urge you to take some food. For it will give you strength, for not a hair is to perish from the head of any of you." And when he had said these things, he took bread, and giving thanks to God in the presence of all he broke it and began to eat. Then they all were encouraged and ate some food themselves. (We were in all 276 persons in the ship.)* (Acts 27:34-37; ESV)

In the presence of all, Paul gave thanks to God. He praised God for the food he had, despite the storm and despite the circumstances. He focused on the promise he received and gave thanks in front of everyone. The result of Paul's gratitude? Scripture says 275 men were left encouraged!

The storm you're in can encourage someone today. Who can you speak to today with your heart of gratitude? Who will be encouraged by your simple act of gratefulness?

DAY 11

GROWTH

There are times in the year we usually think about the faithfulness of God. Gratitude is the best attitude to walk in. As crazy as it sounds, I'm grateful when God stretches me. Why? Because it always brings growth.

Think of a plant that has outgrown its pot. The roots are tangled and squished, and they can't grow to their full potential, right? The only way to allow the plant to grow fully and flourish is to have it replanted in a larger pot. We have to expand its capacity to grow. You see where I'm going, don't you?

If you're hesitant to allow God to expand your capacity by planting you in a larger pot, look what James says:

> *What good is it, my brothers, if someone says he has faith but does not have works? Can that faith save him? If a brother or sister is poorly clothed and lacking in daily food, and one of you says to them, "Go in peace, be warmed and filled," without giving them the things needed for the body, what good is that? So also faith by*

itself, if it does not have works, is dead. (James 2:14-17; ESV)

Let's skip down to verse 26. *"For as the body apart from the spirit is dead, so also faith apart from works is dead."*

If we're still thinking about the plant in the small pot, we can see how preventing growth can cause it to strangle and die. But, the antithesis is growing and flourishing plants when we couple faith and acts of obedience!

Let us be women that keep saying "yes" to God. That keep saying "yes" to getting planted in the bigger pot. The more we say yes, the more those bigger pots become just another pot. We see the faithfulness of God in every pot He moves us into. We know He is making space for us to grow.

I don't know what God is asking you to do, or what areas He wants to stretch you, but you do. Trust Him. Let Him increase your capacity to grow!

DAY 12

KINGDOM BUILDERS

> *Truly, truly, I say to you, whoever believes in me will also do the works that I do; and greater works than these will he do, because I am going to the Father. Whatever you ask in my name, this I will do, that the Father may be glorified in the Son. If you ask me anything in my name, I will do it.* (John 14:12-14; ESV)

We aren't saved by works; we're saved by grace. We know that. But, following Jesus is an action, not a thought. It's not just believing in Him. *"You believe that God is one; you do well. Even the demons believe—and shudder!"* (James 2:19; ESV).

We can't fulfill the purposes of God in our lives if we only "believe in Him." We have to fully surrender our own agendas and link arms with heaven and God's agenda. He will use you to build His kingdom if you let Him.

If you truly believe in Him, you will do works for the kingdom. Because your motive is to bring glory to God. Everything you ask for kingdom building will be done. Jesus wanted to glorify His Father more than anything when He was on earth. And, now that He has given us the Holy Spirit, Jesus says greater works will YOU do. *"Behold, I have given you authority to tread on serpents and scorpions, and over all the power of the enemy, and nothing shall hurt you"* (Luke 10:19; ESV).

You have the authority in Jesus—the Maker of the world—to overcome evil and to build His kingdom.

Raise your faith today friends. Anything you ask in His name WILL be done. You're kingdom builders. You're a woman who fans the flame in His people. You're a woman who says "Yes" to the impossible, because you know you serve a God that demolishes impossibilities.

DAY 13

CONTROL FEAR

Fear. It's a real feeling that can take over one's mind in a hurry if not controlled. We've all been there. You may have even felt fear so strongly that it has stopped you dead in your tracks. It's a distraction the enemy uses a lot on us. We get in fear often times by trying to control life when it's not our position to control.

We have many responsibilities as women, wives, daughters, and moms. And, we've become really good at controlling those responsibilities. After all, our homes run really well when we control different areas God has given us reign over. But, what happens when we start to control (or try to control) the areas He never authorized?

Fear. I find it interesting that God's word shows us how to control fear, when the birth of fear is often started from lack of control. Could it be that God knew we are really good at controlling things He has given us authority over? But, when we try to control the things God has governed, the enemy has a way into our thoughts. To fight against that, God gives us authority to control our minds. What a good God!

> *For though we walk in the flesh, we are not waging war according to the flesh. For the weapons of our warfare are not of the flesh but have divine power to destroy strongholds. We destroy arguments and every lofty opinion raised against the knowledge of God, and take every thought captive to obey Christ, being ready to punish every disobedience, when your obedience is complete.* (2 Corinthians 10:3-6; ESV)

Our weapons of warfare have the power to destroy strongholds. Destroy fear. Demolish lies from the enemy. We must take every thought captive. Those thoughts that try to paralyze us in fear.

After my dad died, I had these strange, random bouts of fear. They came out of nowhere. My husband had to drive up through the mountains a few days after my dad died, and fear gripped me. I was totally fine with him traveling locally. Then all of a sudden, the enemy tried telling me how his life could be taken so quickly traveling up those mountains. The enemy brings torment and fear through situations that cannot be controlled. Through his "lofty opinion raised against the knowledge of God."

But, God has given us tools on how to control those situations that are out of our control.

> *Do not be anxious about anything, but in everything by prayer and supplication with*

> *thanksgiving let your requests be made known to God. And the peace of God, which surpasses all understanding, will guard your hearts and your minds in Christ Jesus.* (Philippians 4:6-7; ESV)

Take every thought captive. Recognize those thoughts. Control them and pray. When you begin taking your thoughts captive and praying, the end result is a peace that will guard your hearts and minds. Isn't that what happens after your quiet time with Jesus? A peace that cannot be explained? Why? Because we stop the thoughts that come against God, and we pray and fix our eyes on His word and truth!

What feels out of control in your life? How can you arrest your thoughts and pray through it instead?

DAY 14

THE FIERY FURNACE

I've mentioned walking through storms, but sometimes a storm doesn't depict the truest form of our despair—the hardship and struggle when we're in the thick of it. Sometimes, a fiery furnace details our season better. But, as followers of Jesus, we know He doesn't leave us in the furnace alone. He promises to never leave us nor forsake us.

Do you remember the story of Shadrach, Meshach, and Abednego? King Nebuchadnezzar made a law in his kingdom that everyone had to bow down and worship some crazy golden idol. Anyone that didn't worship the idol would be thrown into a fiery furnace to die. But, those three men refused. Talk got out, and they were soon summoned to speak to the king and explain themselves.

In verse 15 of chapter 3 in Daniel, the king said, *"And who is the god who will deliver you out of my hands?"* He mocked them thinking they were crazy to not follow his law. They answered King Nebuchadnezzar in verse 17, *"Our God whom we serve IS ABLE to deliver us from the burning fiery furnace."*

Stop there. They knew the promises of God. Their lives were threatened and potential pain stood in their future, but they didn't focus on the furnace. They didn't focus on their situation. They focused on their God and His ABILITY TO DELIVER. The king ordered the furnace to be seven times hotter than it normally was. The three men were thrown into the fire that was so extreme that it took the lives of the guards that threw them in.

A miracle took place that day. An opportunity arose to show the glory of God and who He says He is. The power He holds—even in the midst of the hottest fire. That He is a God that stands with His people—even in the middle of a fiery furnace. Not only did God save those men but THROUGH those men, King Nebuchadnezzar believed in God. The king saw that the three men in the fire were unharmed, shackles were broken off, and a fourth man was in there with them.

> *And the satraps, the prefects, the governors, and the king's counselors gathered together and saw that the fire had not had any power over the bodies of those men. The hair of their heads was not singed, their cloaks were not harmed, and no smell of fire had come upon them.* (Daniel 3:27 ESV)

The fire doesn't have any power over you. Let me say that again. The fire doesn't have any power over you. In fact, even after you're out of the fire you won't have any proof of that fire on your life at all. There isn't any smoke or residue remaining on you. Everyone that sees you walk in the fire, will see that God is with you. And, it will change them and what they believe through you.

> *Nebuchadnezzar answered and said, "Blessed be the God of Shadrach, Meshach, and Abednego, who has sent his angel and delivered his servants, who trusted in him, and set aside the king's command, and yielded up their bodies rather than serve and worship any god except their own God.* (Daniel 3:28 ESV)

Remember, the furnace has no power over you. Instead, God's power is with you. He won't allow any harm to come near you. He is able, and He will deliver you!

DAY 15

CHOOSE YOUR PATH

You know those days when it feels like everywhere you turn, something goes wrong? Getting into your car, you spill your coffee; you get a flat tire on the way to work; you get to work, and you forgot your lunch, etc. As the day progresses, you see one thing after another fall apart. And, in those moments, you have a choice. They're polar opposite choices, but they're both blaring at you to choose them. Do you pick the path of life that feels harder to stand on, or do you pick the easier path that allows you to wallow around and mope about in discouragement? The good news is if you chose the path of wallow, there's a detour to the path of life right where you're standing.

We've all chosen the path of wallow in our lives. But, God is faithful to allow His path of life to be an easy access for us. It's always there, but it's our choice to walk in it.

> *"Thomas said to Him, "Lord, we do not know where You are going, and how can we know the way?" Jesus said to him, "I am the way, the*

> *truth, and the life. No one comes to the Father except through Me"* (John 14:5-6; NKJV).

We don't need to know every turn, fork in the road, or round about ahead. Jesus declares He is the way. He is the path of life. But, before you say, "I've heard this a thousand times," let me show you something. This path of life requires your spirit to become in charge. *"But I say, walk by the Spirit, and you will not gratify the desires of the flesh"* (Galatians 5:16; ESV).

Why must we walk by the Spirit on this path of life? Why can't we choose the path of life and walk in our flesh?

Galatians shows us that by choosing to walk in the spirit, we stop the desires of the flesh. The feelings when we want to wallow around in our flesh bring despair, hopelessness, and discouragement. But, look what happens when you choose to walk in the spirit.

> *But the fruit of the Spirit is love, joy, peace, patience, kindness, goodness, faithfulness, gentleness, self-control; against such things is no law. And those who belong to Christ Jesus have crucified the flesh with its passions and desires."* (Galatians 5:22-24; ESV)

Choose the path of life today, and walk in the spirit. Jesus has promised to give you priceless fruit that can fulfill your life and sustain you from the fleshly desires.

If you feel you have too many problems being thrown at you at once, remember:

> *"When the enemy comes in like a flood, The Spirit of the Lord will lift up a standard against him"* (Isaiah 59:19b; NKJV).

DAY 16

MIRACLES IN OBEDIENCE

---

1 Kings 17

The highlight of this passage is often on Elijah and his obedience, but this time I want to take a closer look at the widow.

> *So he arose and went to Zarephath. And when he came to the gate of the city, behold, a widow was there gathering sticks. And he called to her and said, "Bring me a little water in a vessel, that I may drink." And as she was going to bring it, he called to her and said, "Bring me a morsel of bread in your hand." And she said, "As the Lord your God lives, I have nothing baked, only a handful of flour in a jar and a little oil in a jug. And now I am gathering a couple of sticks that I may go in and prepare it for myself and my son, that we may eat it and die." And Elijah said to her, "Do not fear; go and do as you have said. But first make me a little cake of it and bring it to me, and afterward*

> *make something for yourself and your son. For thus says the Lord, the God of Israel, 'The jar of flour shall not be spent, and the jug of oil shall not be empty, until the day that the Lord sends rain upon the earth.'" And she went and did as Elijah said. And she and he and her household ate for many days. The jar of flour was not spent, neither did the jug of oil become empty, according to the word of the Lord that he spoke by Elijah.* (1 Kings 17:10-16; ESV)

This widow was gathering sticks because her and her son had no food, and she knew her days on earth were nearing an end. Elijah, however, received a command from God back in verse 9 to go looking for a widow that would provide food for him. God said He commanded the widow to provide food for Elijah.

Nowhere in scripture does it explain the widow's point of view when God told her to prepare food for a stranger out of her nothing. But, we see a glimpse of it in her response in verse 12. *"As the Lord your God lives, I have nothing baked, only a handful of flour in a jar and a little oil in a jug…"*

She was at the end of her life, or so she thought. She was preparing to die when God interrupted her with a command that seemed impossible based on her resources. But, out of her lack, she obeyed God. And, the result in verse 16 depicts a miracle because of her obedience! The jar of oil and flour never became empty!

How many moments in our lives have we heard the Holy Spirit tell us to go, or asked us to trust Him in hopeless circumstances?

Could it be He's using your lack to show off His miraculous power in your life? That your story will shine with the faithfulness of God simply because you obeyed when it seemed hopeless?

Let God interrupt you today and watch what He does.

DAY 17

Trust

I have a daughter who is strong willed, determined, and persistent. Often times, I'm having to redirect her and help shape this gift. If you have one of these children, you know that some seasons can be longer than others.

There are many times I will tell her not to do something because it isn't safe, nor the right timing, but she insists on doing it anyway, or doing it her own way. She reasons with me, explains why it will work, and tries her best to convince me. Sometimes, I allow her to try and fail, and other times I will stop her altogether because I know it will end badly.

With this example fresh in your minds, let's read a part in the story of Jonah. When the storm started raging before they threw Jonah overboard, Jonah told them his position with God and why the storm was so intense. Verse 10 tells us the men on the ship knew at that point Jonah was a man of God.

> *Then they said to him, "What shall we do to you, that the sea may quiet down for us?" For the sea grew more and more tempestuous. He said to them, "Pick me up and hurl me into the sea;*

> *then the sea will quiet down for you, for I know it is because of me that this great tempest has come upon you." Nevertheless, the men rowed hard to get back to dry land, but they could not, for the sea grew more and more tempestuous against them.* (Jonah 1:11-13; ESV)

The men asked Jonah for an answer, and he gave it to them. It wasn't what they expected, in fact, they disagreed and tried to do it their own way. They tried rowing back to land, but the storm didn't let them succeed. They strained and fought for who knows how long to do it on their own. It made no sense to them to throw a man into that raging sea.

Have there been times in your life when God has asked you to do something that makes zero sense? Or maybe times when you think you can solve a problem on your own because you're certain it will work without needing the Holy Spirit's guidance?

God was faithful in this story. He spared every man's life, including Jonah's. And, because of the men's reckless faith in God, they did hurl Jonah into the sea, and the end result was in verse 16, *"Then the men feared the Lord exceedingly, and they offered a sacrifice to the Lord and made vows."*

The men feared God in a new way that day. It wasn't fear as in being scared. Rather, it was fear that held a high level of honoring respect. Not only did Jonah's life completely change, but so did the men on that ship.

God knows the whole story. The end result. Every time. Trust His leading, His prompting, His instructions. They may sound silly, or completely ridiculous, but God knows the glory that will happen if you trust and obey. *"Trust in the Lord with all your heart, and do not lean on your own understanding. In all your ways acknowledge him, and he will make straight your paths"* (Proverbs 3:5-6; ESV).

DAY 18

HOPE

When I hear this word hope, I often think of Abraham and Sara. God had promised him so much, but there was a waiting period before Abraham saw the promise manifest.

So, how do we keep our hope when we're in the waiting period? The season of lack, waiting, brokenness with sorrow, or even emptiness? Let's look in Hebrews to see what God says about hope.

> *For when God made a promise to Abraham, since he had no one greater by whom to swear, he swore by himself, saying, "Surely I will bless you and multiply you." And thus Abraham, having patiently waited, obtained the promise.*
> (Hebrews 6:13–15; ESV)

Patience is something that no one asks for but something we all need! While patience is a key component to waiting, there's something greater. Look at verse 19.

> *"We have this as a sure and steadfast anchor of the soul, a hope that enters into the inner place behind the curtain…"* (Hebrews 6:19; ESV).

There it is. We can still get to the promise without being patient, but we all know grumbling and complaining could make us go around the mountain a few more times than we're supposed to. The way we receive hope is by spending time with Jesus. When we spend time behind the curtain He does something new in our hearts and in our spirits. Hope resides with Jesus. The more time we spend with Him, the more we align our hearts with His.

> *"You will seek me and find me, when you seek me with all your heart"* (Jeremiah 29:13; ESV).

We find Jesus. The real heart of Jesus when we seek Him with our everything.

> *"For I know the plans I have for you, declares the Lord, plans for welfare and not for evil, to give you a future and a hope"* (Jeremiah 29:11; ESV).

He knows the future and the plans for us. During the waiting for those plans to manifest, He tells us where our hope is found. And, He promises that He will give it to us! If you're feeling hopeless or not as full as you want, spend time behind the curtain today. Watch how He fills you.

DAY 19

GET AWAY

Have you ever needed to get away to a place of solitude with just you and Jesus? A time set aside to seek Him and hear what He has wanted to tell you? I love the mountains. There's something about getting away to a place that isn't highly traveled and populated. I tend to believe I can hear better when I get away, and I get revelations and words from God.

Look what Paul did when he got a revelation from God.

> *For I did not receive it from any man, nor was I taught it, but I received it through a revelation of Jesus Christ. For you have heard of my former life in Judaism, how I persecuted the church of God violently and tried to destroy it. And I was advancing in Judaism beyond many of my own age among my people, so extremely zealous was I for the traditions of my fathers. But when he who had set me apart before I was born, and who called me by his grace, was pleased to reveal his Son to me, in order that I might preach him among the Gentiles, I did*

> *not immediately consult with anyone; nor did I go up to Jerusalem to those who were apostles before me, but I went away into Arabia, and returned again to Damascus."* (Galatians 1:12-17; ESV)

You too are set apart and called by His grace, and He is pleased to reveal Himself to you. Oh, how it brings Him such joy when you spend time with Him. He has much to tell you daughter. He has set you apart to hear His revelation that is hand-picked for you.

When Paul received the revelation, he didn't go into the familiar city where Jesus' disciples were. It probably would have been easy to talk to the men that walked with Jesus and touched Jesus. It probably would have been helpful to pick their brains on how this King spoke to His people. But instead, Paul "went away."

Paul spent time alone with the Holy Spirit for three years. Chewing on the words God spoke to him and the revelations he was getting. He got his heart right and his mission clear. He relied on the Holy Spirit to show him what he was called to do. Why he was set apart. What his position in the kingdom was.

Even Jesus knew the importance of getting away. *"And rising very early in the morning, while it was still dark, he departed and went out to a desolate place, and there he prayed"* (Mark 1:35; ESV).

Have you spent time alone with God recently? Whether you've gotten a specific word or not, you're set apart. You've been called. I challenge you to wait on the revelation He gives you and get away. Whether it's your closet, bathroom, shower, or the few moments you have while preparing dinner.

Get away with the Holy Spirit, and let Him show you what He has called you to this season. It will be of great worth. All for His glory.

DAY 20

PROCLAIM HIS NAME

And I will vindicate the holiness of my great name, which has been profaned among the nations, and which you have profaned among them. And the nations will know that I am the Lord, declares the Lord God, when through you I vindicate my holiness before their eyes.

And I will give you a new heart, and a new spirit I will put within you. And I will remove the heart of stone from your flesh and give you a heart of flesh. And I will put my Spirit within you and cause you to walk in my statutes and be careful to obey my rules. (Ezekiel 36:23, 26-27; ESV)

Even though I never persecuted God's church like Saul, I was still a sinful woman. I used to live a life that was unpleasant to God and even caused a stench that I gagged on. It is God that changes the heart of men and women. Not by anything of our own doing. He seeks us out. Listen to those words. He sought you out.

> *For thus says the Lord God: Behold, I, I myself will search for my sheep and will seek them out. As a shepherd seeks out his flock when he is among his sheep that have been scattered, so will I seek out my sheep, and I will rescue them from all places where they have been scattered on a day of clouds and thick darkness.*
>
> *I will seek the lost, and I will bring back the strayed, and I will bind up the injured, and I will strengthen the weak...* (Ezekiel 34:11-12, 16a; ESV)

He brought us out. Maybe He's still bringing you out. Maybe He's saving you from a destructive path, a chaotic lifestyle, or one similar to mine. Either way, it is for His Name to be proclaimed! The end of verse 23 in chapter 36 says, *"And the nations will know that I am the Lord, declares the Lord God, when through you I vindicate my holiness before their eyes."*

Your story, your injuries, your sin will be turned around for good and declare His holiness among the nations. Your "nation" is right where you live. Use your story to bring Him glory.

Even though Ezekiel was receiving this word for Israel, it is for us as well. *"For whatever was written in former days was written for our instruction, that through endurance and through the encouragement of the Scriptures we might have hope"* (Romans 15:4; ESV).

Has your hope increased today knowing that you get to play a role in God's kingdom? This is your season to proclaim His name. To tell the nations of His goodness! He sought you out. He is restoring your life to align with His. All to tell the nations of His goodness, and He's using you to proclaim His Name.

DAY 21

LITTLE FAITH

Isn't it funny that we can be so confident and full of faith one minute, but the circumstances in our world can change our thoughts in an instant? There are times I feel like I have multiple personalities! Do you ever feel the same? Sometimes, I'm on my "A game" and call out those things that aren't as though they are. But, at other times, when one small hiccup appears in my world, and I feel like my life is over.

What gives me comfort is that the disciples were literally walking next to Jesus, touching Him, smelling Him, and physically seeing Him perform miracle after miracle, yet they had moments of worry. Moments of doubt. But, Jesus still chose them. He knew they were of little faith when He called them. He knew they would waver and freak out when circumstances arose. But, He also knew He could use them in the midst of their storms for greatness.

> *And behold, there arose a great storm on the sea, so that the boat was being swamped by the waves; but he was asleep. And they went and woke him, saying, "Save us, Lord; we are*

> *perishing." And he said to them, "Why are you afraid, O you of little faith?" Then he rose and rebuked the winds and the sea, and there was a great calm. And the men marveled, saying, "What sort of man is this, that even winds and sea obey him?"* (Matthew 8:24-27; ESV)

Jesus didn't say to the disciples, "You guys! You have zero faith." Instead He said "little faith." He knew they had a little faith. The disciples felt like they were about to die. They called out to God, "Save us, Lord; we are perishing!" They saw their circumstances change. Even though they witnessed God's miracle just a few days before with Jesus healing a leper!

How many times in our lives do we remember the faithfulness of God from the time before, but we still need the assurance that He will do it again? Can I tell you that's okay? He knows our faith isn't perfect. He knows we need assurance, and He will give it to you again.

Jesus wasn't surprised at the disciples or angry that they woke Him up. He didn't yell at them and say, "Figure it out for yourself. I just showed you a miracle a few days ago." Instead, He rose up, rebuked the storm, and calmed the winds.

It's okay to ask for help in a storm. It doesn't mean you have zero faith. It means you know who holds the answer. Don't get hung up on where you hoped your faith level would be, but rather focus on the fact you knew to cry out to Jesus.

"But you, O Lord, are a shield about me, my glory, and the lifter of my head. I cried aloud to the Lord, and he answered me from his holy hill. Selah" (Psalms 3:3-4; ESV).

DAY 22

IDLE

Have you ever had moments or seasons where you feel you're just idling? Sitting there exhausting your resources of fuel but not moving? Your car is all nice and warm inside, your foot waiting to move from the brake to the gas, but you still have the red light and an almost empty tank of gas now? A dream God has given you, but you're still idling—on the almost fumes now waiting for the "go ahead"?

Remember what Paul told the Galatians in chapter 6: *"And let us not grow weary of doing good, for in due season we will reap, if we do not give up"* (Galatians 6:9; ESV).

There are times we all are ready to throw in the towel and give up on the dream God gave us. Perhaps you're in the middle of that dream now, but you haven't seen the fruit. If we're not careful, our souls become weary, and we start believing the enemy and his lies when he whispers, "You didn't hear right. Just quit now. You're wasting gas. Look at what you could be doing with your life if you quit."

But, what if while you're sitting there idling, God wants you to see something? See something you would have missed if you had been driving? What if that person on the side of the road you noticed will meet Jesus through your smile? Through your testimony? Through your compassion? What if your relationship with Jesus soars in this season because you're able to sit and listen to Him while you're waiting?

In chapter 6, Paul talks about bearing each other's burdens and staying in step together for Jesus. The last verse of the chapter and the verse that follows the one we just read says,

> *"So then, as we have opportunity, let us do good to everyone, and especially to those who are of the household of faith"* (Galatians 6:10; ESV).

Those opportunities will only come if we're looking for them. Don't get discouraged when you're idling. It's an opportunity for the Holy Spirit to use you. And, when we keep pursuing Him and keep pursuing the dream, we will reap because we didn't give up.

Idling reminds us to *"Be still and know that I am God"* (Psalm 46:10a). Without that reminder we tend to try and help God with the details. We try to get out of the car and start pushing it when it's in park. But, it is often in those moments of waiting and idling that we hear Him ever so clearly. It's in those times that we are led to tears because we can hear His voice so tenderly. If you are in a season of fatigue and burn-out, take some time to sit and be still. Just be in His presence, and allow His still small voice to bring you strength.

DAY 23

HOLY

Remember the story of David bringing the ark to Jerusalem? His army had just defeated the Philistines by the power of God and thirty thousand men were celebrating. They had placed the ark on a new cart and were making their journey to Jerusalem with singing and playing instruments. But, then something went wrong.

> *But when they arrived at the threshing floor of Nacon, the oxen stumbled, and Uzzah reached out his hand and steadied the Ark of God. Then the Lord's anger was aroused against Uzzah, and God struck him dead because of this. So Uzzah died right there beside the Ark of God. David was angry because the Lord's anger had burst out against Uzzah. He named that place Perez-uzzah (which means "to burst out against Uzzah"), as it is still called today. David was now afraid of the Lord, and he asked, "How can I ever bring the Ark of the Lord back into my care?" So David decided not to move the*

> *Ark of the Lord into the City of David. Instead, he took it to the house of Obed-edom of Gath.*
> (2 Samuel 6:6-10; NLT)

David wasn't supposed to transport the ark on a cart. Those instructions were given to Moses long ago. The ark was supposed to be carried on Levite's shoulders with poles. Scripture tells us that the ark stayed at Abinadab's house, which was Uzzah's dad. Did Uzzah get too familiar with the ark? Did he stop honoring it the way it was meant to be honored? Did he no longer see it as holy and sacred?

This stood out to me. The longer we walk with Jesus, the more comfortable we get. And in a way, we should. He's a Father that loves us and longs for our hearts. He longs to have a relationship with us. But, in that relationship, have you gotten too comfortable that you've lost sight of how Holy Jesus is?

If your perception of Jesus has been dumbed down because of familiarity, I challenge you to reposition your thoughts of His power and His Holiness.

> *"Great is the Lord, and greatly to be praised; And His greatness is unsearchable"* (Psalms 145:3; NKJV).

> *"Great is our Lord, and abundant in power; his understanding is beyond measure"* (Psalms 147:5; ESV).

Holy, Holy, Holy is the Lord!

DAY 24

THE TRAP OF PRIDE

When you hear the word humility, what do you think of? Meek, kind, putting others first? What does God's word say about it?

> "But he gives more grace. Therefore it says, 'God opposes the proud but gives grace to the humble'" (James 4:6; ESV).

Some translations say God resists the proud. If we know God is against pride and behaviors that reflect pride, why do we cling to it? Why do we hide behind it thinking we gain protection from it?

I've hung onto pride many times, because I thought that if I was humble, I could get hurt more easily. That the sting of rejection would be lessened if my pride was puffed up from the start. But, does that rejection hurt less when we attach our hope in pride? I think we know the answer.

But, if we believed what scripture actually says, we would understand grace covers it all. In fact, James tells us God gives more grace.

Finding Strength in the Pursuit

I've battled with rejection. After I experienced it, my fleshly response was to reject back. It's more comfortable for me to put up a wall of pride for protection than it is to humble myself or "humiliate" myself.

Wait. Are those two words the same?

Humiliate is a negative attribute to humility. Scripture isn't asking us to humiliate ourselves. It's asking us to think of ourselves less. C.S. Lewis said, "True humility is not thinking less of yourself, it is thinking of yourself less." [1]

When I'm offended and hurt, it's because I'm focused on my feelings and what my needs are. When someone doesn't respond like I'd hoped, it's because I'm thinking about how that person can fill my bucket. But, God doesn't ask us to rely on others to fill us. He's tells us to come to Him to have our buckets filled.

> *"Come to me, all who labor and are heavy laden, and I will give you rest"* (Matthew 11:28 ESV).

Rest from our hurts, our rejections, our insecurities. He gives us rest when we come to Him. When we stop placing the hope in others, and we put our hope in Him.

> *"Humble yourselves, therefore, under the mighty hand of God so that at the proper time he may*

---

[1] C.S. Lewis, *Mere Christianity* (NewYork: MacMillan Pub. Co., 1952), 128.

exalt you, casting all your anxieties on him, because he cares for you" (1 Peter 5:6-7; ESV).

He cares for you more than any human on the planet does. Jesus came and gave Himself fully knowing the rejection He would receive. Fully knowing the weight of humility that He must embrace, yet never receiving the love back to Him that He deserved. But, He still did it.

When you come to a place of rejection, remember to take it to God. Spend time with Him, and allow Him to change your perspective and give you rest from your thoughts. Don't build up walls of pride. *"Humble yourselves before the Lord, and he will lift you up in honor"* (James 4:10; NLT).

What offense do you have today that you can take to God? What areas of your life have you put up a wall to falsely protect yourself? Choose humility today, and let God lift you up.

DAY 25

FAITHFULNESS

I like to watch movies that I've already seen. The ones that tug on my heart strings and end with some form of happily ever after. The ones that I can ugly cry in the middle, yet have hope at the same time, because I know how it ends.

The death, burial, and resurrection story pulls on every fiber in my being. I read scripture that depicts what Jesus went through for His people. I watch movies that portray the anguish He endured to bring freedom to the world, yet I know the end of the story. I know that His death wasn't in vain. It was with great purpose, and He rose from the grave and is now alive and seated at the right-hand throne of God.

I got to thinking about that. If we know what happens and we believe it to be true, this selfless act of love portrayed by our Messiah, why don't we always believe it to be true for our own lives?

Maybe we're afraid.

> "He isn't here! He is risen from the dead, just as he said would happen. Come, see where his body was lying. And now, go quickly and tell

> *his disciples that he has risen from the dead, and he is going ahead of you to Galilee. You will see him there. Remember what I have told you." The women ran quickly from the tomb. They were very frightened but also filled with great joy, and they rushed to give the disciples the angel's message. And as they went, Jesus met them and greeted them. And they ran to him, grasped his feet, and worshiped him. Then Jesus said to them, "Don't be afraid! Go tell my brothers to leave for Galilee, and they will see me there."* (Matthew 28:6-10; NLT)

Those women just had an encounter with an angel who told them Jesus had risen just as He said He would. The angel told them not to be afraid in verse 5 but urged them to go quickly to tell the disciples of this good news. But, he gave them a promise: *"Jesus is going ahead of you."* Sure enough, Jesus met them there and greeted them when they arrived!

What if they would have allowed their fear to keep them from obeying?

Jesus knew they were afraid, but He proved His faithfulness to them so they could carry on with the mission. Matthew's description of this is beautiful. Once the women arrived in Galilee, Jesus was there, just as He said he would be. He showed His faithfulness to them and told them to tell his brothers to go to Galilee and they would see Him.

Faithfulness

The faithfulness of God isn't dependent on our obedience. Jesus would have been there just as He said He would, even if the women didn't conquer their fear.

But, look at the legacy they left because of their obedience. They showed us how to tackle fear. Run your race daughter, knowing Jesus will meet you where He called you.

DAY 26

THE WORD

If I could give credit to any one specific account in my life, it would be the habit of reading the Bible. It has formed my thoughts and renewed my thinking. Yes, God has changed my heart to align with His, but it has been the word of God that has redefined my thoughts. My discerning. Even my interpretation of life and events.

> *For the word of God is living and active, sharper than any two-edged sword, piercing to the division of soul and of spirit, of joints and of marrow, and discerning the thoughts and intentions of the heart.* (Hebrews 4:12; ESV)

This passage is powerful to me. Not only does the word of God penetrate and pierce our thoughts and our spirit, but it also pierces us physically. It defines what our genetic makeup actually is! Every joint and every marrow. The marrow is the inner soft part of the bone where all of the blood is brought and supplied to the bones. It is where the bones receive the nutrients and energy to sustain its purpose.

That's what scripture does! It receives the blood to fulfill its purpose. Hold on. This gets even better! Look at John.

> *In the beginning was the Word, and the Word was with God, and the Word was God. He was in the beginning with God.* (John 1:1-2; ESV)

> *And the Word became flesh and dwelt among us, and we have seen his glory, glory as of the only Son from the Father, full of grace and truth.* (John 1:14; ESV)

The blood of Jesus is running through your very body. Your genetic makeup was created by God to fulfill His purposes for you in your life. Your purpose is supplied and sustained by the word. That's how we receive our nutrients.

The word of God became flesh and dwelt on earth. Jesus. He died to give you abundant life!

The blood is within you, and greater is He who is in you than he (Satan) who is in the world. (1 John 4:4)

It's no wonder we hear scripture and something in us awakens, leaps, perks up. Why? Because it's what you're made of!

If you want to know who you are and be redefined by why you were born, read God's word daily. Let it speak to your inner being and realign your thoughts with God's original plan for your life. It's sharper than a sword, it penetrates and pierces every single thing and accomplishes what it was sent to do. (Hebrews 4:12)

DAY 27

PASSION OR PERFECTION?

I have a tendency to strive for perfection. It's gotten better over the years as I've allowed the Holy Spirit to teach me, but it still creeps up every now and then. My daughter isn't a perfectionist, but when it comes to soccer, she often plays as though she has to achieve perfection. My husband and I are constantly saying, "We're not asking for perfection; we're asking for your passion."

Let me explain. If we allow perfection to drive us, we will always fall short. God didn't make us perfect beings, but He did impart passions within us to be used to fulfill His plans for us. We mustn't allow the enemy to twist our passion into perfection or performance.

> *"Whatever you do, work heartily, as for the Lord and not for men"* (Colossians 3:23; ESV).

In the story of Daniel and the lion's den, we read that God protected him. No harm came to him the entire time he was in the den. But, early in the story we learn about Daniel and his character.

> *Then the high officials and the satraps sought to find a ground for complaint against Daniel with regard to the kingdom, but they could find no ground for complaint or any fault, because he was faithful, and no error or fault was found in him.* (Daniel 6:4; ESV)

Did you catch why Daniel was different? He was faithful. Faithful in what God had given him authority over. Faithful in the everyday tasks that he faced.

A Godly passion will strengthen us to remain faithful. A Godly passion will sustain you into faithfulness. Don't worry about the details or even the outcome. Just remain faithful in what God has given you. He hasn't asked us for perfection. He knows us too well and knows we will always fall short, but He does ask us to remain faithful.

> *"Blessed is the man who remains steadfast under trial, for when he has stood the test he will receive the crown of life, which God has promised to those who love him"* (James 1:12; ESV).

You will receive the crown of life as you remain faithful and steadfast. His promises for you are greater than any achievement of perfection you try to strive for. Let us show off our God-given passions!

DAY 28

Our Hearts

I think I learn more as an adult after having kids than before I did! If you're a mom, do you find yourself learning more when your children walk through struggles and trials? As we begin to teach them principles, the Holy Spirit shows us where our hearts are. Even if we don't listen to Him, our words will show us what our hearts are full of.

> *"The good person out of the good treasure of his heart produces good, and the evil person out of his evil treasure produces evil, for out of the abundance of the heart his mouth speaks"* (Luke 6:45; ESV).

Is your natural response to speak encouragement or to tear down? Is your first response to yell? Is your first action to call up someone to rant or tell them your latest issue? What is your heart so full of that you hear it spilling out of your mouth?

My children are normal kids. They have days that they're so sweet and kind to each other and other days they're close to Satan's offspring! But, something that is consistent is the reason for their evil behaviors. Their hearts and buckets are filled with stuff they were never intended to be filled with. Too much TV, video games, coveting a neighbor's toy, or other material things leads them to a heart full of the flesh. When I don't give them enough attention or speak God's truth over them, I notice these behaviors take shape.

Isn't that true of us? When we aren't spending time with Jesus, our hearts will become full of something else. Whatever it is we're spending time on is what shapes the outpouring of our mouths. Are you spending time filling your heart with God's word, His truth, and His love so you can't help but speak those things out? Or is your attention on things that don't truly matter? Things that occupy your time and suck your heart of the very thing that was meant to sustain you?

Spend some time asking the Holy Spirit to show you what areas in your heart have been filled by something or someone that was meant to be filled by Jesus and Him alone.

DAY 29

USE YOUR VOICE

Do you remember the story of Joseph? He was having dreams and was telling his brothers and father about the dreams. Only the brothers didn't like what Joseph was saying. They didn't like what he was foretelling, so they plotted against him. They sold him after throwing him into a pit with the intent to kill him.

> *But when Reuben heard it, he rescued him out of their hands, saying, "Let us not take his life." And Reuben said to them, "Shed no blood; throw him into this pit here in the wilderness, but do not lay a hand on him"—that he might rescue him out of their hand to restore him to his father.* (Genesis 37:21-22; ESV)

I want to examine the aspect of silence in this passage. The brothers wanted to throw him into a pit so they wouldn't hear Joseph speak these prophetic plans. They wanted to stop his voice from proclaiming God's plans. Sound similar to what the enemy does to you? Has the enemy ever tried to silence your voice by throwing you into a pit?

> *"And they took him and threw him into a pit. The pit was empty; there was no water in it"* (Genesis 37:24; ESV).

Sometimes, the pit we find ourselves in is empty and without water, but Jesus is always with us. He is our living water. Our voice is a weapon against the enemy!

Scripture doesn't tell us what Joseph prayed, thought, or suffered in the pit. But he was a man of God, and I imagine he spoke to God while in that pit. Your voice and your prayers are powerful! They cause the demons to flee, and whatever you bind and loose on earth will be bound and loosed in heaven.

If you're in a pit today, don't let the enemy keep you from using your voice. Speak out loud today the goodness of God. Proclaim it over your life and your family. Praise God for His faithfulness. You wear the crown of life, and your lineage is in Jesus!

DAY 30

FAN YOUR FLAME

> *"For this reason I remind you to fan into flame the gift of God, which is in you through the laying on of my hands"* (2 Timothy 1:6; ESV).

Have you ever tried to start a campfire? Like, the old fashion way? Not with a lighter or some other twentieth century means. But with a couple sticks and some kindling? You know how purposeful you have to be in the beginning before the flame catches? You have to be right in there. Your knees are bent; you're crouched over, both hands at work, and your face is right there. As soon as you see a spark you blow on it in hopes that the flame will ignite.

This is how we are to be with the gifts God has given us. Purposeful. Relentless. Consistent. If we don't practice the gifts we have, they will lose their flame. Paul is explaining how we must fan the flame God has given us so that it doesn't go out.

Look at the verse prior to the one we just read. *"I am reminded of your sincere faith, a faith that dwelt first in your grandmother Lois and your mother Eunice and now, I am sure, dwells in you as well"* (2 Timothy 1:5 ; ESV).

Normally, we pass on by with these types of verses. But, think about what Paul is suggesting. Timothy had a grandmother and a mother who were full of faith and paved the way for Timothy through their own lives. But, perhaps Paul is urging Timothy not to put his hope in that just because of their efforts, he can just breeze on by. But, that he too must fan the flame in order to continue on the path his ancestors created for him.

Do you ever rely on others to pray for you instead of with you to teach you or encourage you? To put your hope in them to carry you through life? Paul is telling us we must fan our own flame. Practice the gifts God has given us. Be purposeful and relentless in our pursuit.

We don't have to worry we're not good enough, smart enough, or strong enough. God's word tells us He will do it!

"He who calls you is faithful; he will surely do it" (1 Thessalonians 5:24; ESV).

Be confident today that He who began a good work in you, will bring it to its full completion. What areas in your life do you need to start blowing on the embers that haven't ignited yet?

Conclusion

The theme we see all throughout scripture is the relentless pursuit of love that God shows to His people. Jesus exemplified what it meant to fully pursue the assignment of extravagant love to the world. How did He find strength during His pursuit? The gospels depict the hidden strength was found knowing how loved He was by His Father, His time in prayer with His Father, and knowing scripture.

If we first know that we are loved more than anything by our Creator, we will have the confidence to continue on our race. If we spend time each day praying and allowing the Holy Spirit to speak to us, we will establish an intimate relationship with Jesus that is essential for every believer. He will give us a strength that will sustain us to fulfill our life-long journey. If you add the written word of God into that equation, you will be able to gain strength from every depiction of struggle displayed and how God's sovereign hand leads us through it all.

My life displays the constant struggles, storms, and heartaches that the world longs to offer. However, God's beauty is spoken louder and shines brighter in it all. I've learned that the mystery of overcoming those struggles is directly connected to Jesus. He is my strength in those issues of life. He is my strength in the pursuit, and He can be yours too.

Acknowledgments

Thank you "small group ladies" for being an encouragement through every season of my life. You all are true examples of finding strength in the pursuit. I am grateful for every single one of you.

Jennifer Barth, you have been such a loyal friend. You've cheered me on every step of the way. You've helped me see that with God nothing is impossible! I love you beyond words and am forever grateful for that day you asked me to lead a small group with you. What an adventure we have been on!

My tribe. You're God's gift to me and my family. You love us through the good and the bad, and I love each of you deeply. Thank you for doing life with us and giving us a family we can call our own. I have the best moments with you, in town and out of town; with and without pie.

Thank you Capital Church, for being a rich soil where my roots can go deep. Where my family can grow and flourish in the house. I'm so grateful for a community of believers that are sold out for Jesus and love people well.

Notes

Day 24: The Trap of Pride

1. C.S. Lewis, *Mere Christianity* (New York: MacMillan Pub. Co., 1952), 128.